A HEART IN PIECES

A Journey from Grief to Grace

Ryan –
There are no
words, but love
and memories will
sustain us – ♡

Barbara Jo Almendinger

Barbara J. Almendinger

WESTBOW
PRESS®
A DIVISION OF THOMAS NELSON
& ZONDERVAN

This book is a work of non-fiction. Unless otherwise noted, the author and the publisher make no explicit guarantees as to the accuracy of the information contained in this book and in some cases, names of people and places have been altered to protect their privacy.

Scripture taken from the Holy Bible, NEW INTERNATIONAL VERSION®. Copyright © 1973, 1978, 1984 by Biblica, Inc. All rights reserved worldwide. Used by permission. NEW INTERNATIONAL VERSION® and NIV® are registered trademarks of Biblica, Inc. Use of either trademark for the offering of goods or services requires the prior written consent of Biblica US, Inc.

WestBow Press books may be ordered through booksellers or by contacting:

WestBow Press
A Division of Thomas Nelson & Zondervan
1663 Liberty Drive
Bloomington, IN 47403
www.westbowpress.com
1 (866) 928-1240

Because of the dynamic nature of the Internet, any web addresses or links contained in this book may have changed since publication and may no longer be valid. The views expressed in this work are solely those of the author and do not necessarily reflect the views of the publisher, and the publisher hereby disclaims any responsibility for them.

Any people depicted in stock imagery provided by Thinkstock are models, and such images are being used for illustrative purposes only. Certain stock imagery © Thinkstock.

ISBN: 978-1-5127-4012-7 (sc)
ISBN: 978-1-5127-4013-4 (hc)
ISBN: 978-1-5127-4011-0 (e)

Library of Congress Control Number: 2016906797

Print information available on the last page.

WestBow Press rev. date: 05/18/2016

CONTENTS

ACKNOWLEDGMENTS

A Heart in Pieces would not have been written if not for the gentle, persistent nudging and encouragement of so many special friends. Thank you for your unwavering friendship, faith, and depth of understanding you have shared with me about extreme loss and God's love.

People who have experienced such sudden, devastating loss share a depth of understanding that others who haven't cannot grasp. Thank you to these special friends who also experienced this kind of loss for opening your hearts to me. There were so many willing to embark on this journey of healing together. What a blessing you all have been as you shared God's love and its ability to heal all hurts when I needed it most.

Thank you, Sherri Somers, for the many hours you poured into helping and supporting me with this book from beginning to end. I could not have completed this endeavor without the valuable insight you offered. Your giving heart is an inspiration to so many. Thank you to the many friends and family who proofread and offered constructive, encouraging words along the way. A special thank you to my mom and dad; I love you both. Without your love and encouragement, this book would never have been possible. I especially want to thank my boys, David and Jeremy, for supporting me along this journey. What a blessing you both are to me.

A special thank you goes to my pastor, Kevin Heckathorn, for helping me find my way back from the pain and brokenness and into the loving arms of God. Thank you also for the numerous hours you spent reading my drafts and providing valuable feedback.

I would also like to acknowledge the many medical professionals who guided me as I searched for answers. Thank you to Dr. Kosnic, from Nationwide Children's Hospital, for spear-heading the fact-finding meeting that provided the valuable insight I needed.

—To Mary K and Mary,
Always in my heart.

INTRODUCTION

If you are reading this book, you most likely have experienced loss in some form or another. Please know that my heart goes out to you. As you search for comfort and answers amidst your suffering, and as you read my book, know there is not a guide book, a quick solution, or an easy fix to healing from loss. *A Heart in Pieces* is not a step-by-step guide on how to get through loss. Nor is it an all-inclusive answer booklet that will fix your broken heart. It is instead a message from my heart to yours, a message from which I hope you can pull an idea and take comfort. My desire for you is that you will find hope, from one survivor to another, and move one step closer to healing. True healing comes from deep within each one of us, and with God's help, it is possible.

1

THIS WAS ONLY THE BEGINNING

Life is a journey, not a destination.

—Ralph Waldo Emerson

High school is considered the time of your life. Ideally, you are carefree, worry free, and making the most of each moment. Days consist of who is dating whom, extra-curricular activities, sporting events, practices, homework, and hanging out with friends. It is that time in life when you should not have a serious worry in the world. The first few months of my senior year were as I just described, very typical, much like any other year in high school—except that it was the much anticipated senior year, the last hoorah, the best year of my high school life.

November 22, 1986, was a typical fall Saturday in Ohio. Ohio State was playing Michigan, so nearly everyone in the entire state had donned the scarlet and gray. I was a high school cheerleader, and that night was the first basketball game of the season. I went to the game, cheered, had fun, and drove home thinking about meeting friends later for pizza. I was the youngest of three children. My parents had three kids in three years, which at times may have seemed completely insane. At this point, I was the only child left in high school; my parents were about to cross the parenting finish line. I am sure they were anticipating lots more free time and a great sense of relief.

When I got home that Saturday night, there was a note on the family room table from my parents: "We went to the hospital; your sister had another seizure. We will call and let you know when we know something." My older sister, Mary K, had been diagnosed with a mild form of epilepsy when she was young. She had these fainting spells every so often, so the note from my parents was no great cause for concern. I decided to go have dinner with a friend, and arrived home around 10 p.m. From the minute I walked in the door, life as I knew it would change forever.

My sister—twenty years old, married, and a new mother with a five week-old baby—was dead. How could this happen? Apparent cause of death: a heart attack. My sister had lain down to take a nap that Saturday evening and just died. She was healthy; I had just seen her that afternoon as we crossed paths at our parents' house. I was heading out to my basketball game, and she was stopping by to visit with our parents. I remember thinking, *This isn't possible. This can't be happening. This has to be a bad dream.* My big sister, the one I looked up to, admired, wanted to be just like, was gone forever. Mary K and I had shared a room my entire life, fought like sisters typically do, shared clothes, tears, and advice about boyfriends. How could she be gone in an instant—just like that? This was way beyond anything my teenage mind could possibly comprehend.

Most of the next week was a complete blur, except for a few indelible snapshot moments in time burned into my memory forever. I will never forget the sound of my mom throwing up all night long after they got home from the hospital. I vividly remember the calling hours with the long line of friends and family. I remember the receiving line with my brother at my side, supporting me, often elbowing me to keep it together, especially when certain persons offering condolences caused me to fall to pieces. I recall my mother screaming and wailing at the funeral home as we said goodbye and closed the casket for the very last time, followed by my dad prying my mother off my sister's casket at the cemetery as the graveside service concluded. Another recollection from that day was time with family and friends back at the house, fondly remembering my sister, and the many ornery stunts we pulled growing up. These are the snapshots I recall from some thirty years ago. It still feels as if they happened yesterday.

My parents were too grief-stricken to even think about functioning, let alone making decisions, plus now they had a new grandbaby to help care for. The task of going through Mary K's clothes and personal belongings fell to me—three weeks shy of my eighteenth birthday—and her best friend, Lori. We boxed up her clothes and personal belongings the day after her funeral. I went into autopilot mode, knowing this difficult job had to be done because no one else was able to tackle the gut-wrenching task. I think my heart was too overwhelmed to feel, so I did what needed to be done to help my family in this way.

The very next day was Thanksgiving. How could we find something to be thankful for? Our family was reeling in grief and sorrow. A tidal wave of disbelief, heartache, and longing not to have to face this harsh reality hit me; my sister was gone—forever. We were all thrust so suddenly into the depths of sorrow and confusion, not knowing how to even begin to make sense of this devastating blow just dealt to us. How could we face our first holiday so soon after my sister's death?

The burdens associated with death kept mounting. Even after a year had passed, still coping with their overwhelming grief, my parents could not bring themselves to take care of the many decisions associated with the death of their daughter. A year after Mary K's death, the task of ordering her headstone fell to me. This decision was just too painful for my parents to endure. What does an eighteen-year-old college freshman know about ordering a headstone? Nothing at all. But I knew they needed me, and honestly, it helped me feel I was doing something for my sister—a tribute to her, so to speak. I wanted to take care of her as she had done for me growing up. Doing something, doing anything, gave me the feeling I was moving forward, working through my grief.

The gaping hole that my sister's death left in our once-intact family of five knocked us all off our feet. Unfortunately, when faced with a sudden and unexpected death, one can only do so much at the time to process the intense sadness of the loss. Working our way out of the darkness of the grief that enveloped our family was mostly accomplished by focusing our energy onto her newborn son. Having her son close to us, knowing he was a part of her, gave us some comfort during a time when comfort was not easy to come by. No one would ever replace her, but my nephew did wonders to soothe our aching hearts.

Why did God let this happen? This is the universal question people tend to ask when faced with unplanned, unexpected loss. We were a good family who went to church every Sunday in the small town where we lived. My parents had been youth group leaders from the time I was twelve. We went on a church mission trip every summer. The mission trips were spent working hard, learning about service to others who are less fortunate, having fun with friends, and studying the Word of God. Wasn't God supposed to show his love by sparing families like ours from tragedies like these? This is exactly how I had thought in my naïve teenage mind before my sister was taken from us so suddenly. Following Mary K's death, I began to think we had fooled ourselves into believing if we just lived a godly life, God would look favorably on us and spare us from tragedies like this.

Many well-meaning friends and family kept using the hollow phrases, "God works in mysterious ways," or "God doesn't give you more than you can handle," in an attempt to offer us comfort in our time of need and to help us make sense of this terrible tragedy. As a lost and mourning teenager, there was little comfort in those words. I was part of the "God loves me and protects me from harm" crowd. At eighteen, I wanted no part of "God does not give you more than you can handle." It only added to my frustration and confusion as I tried to wrap my mind around spending the rest of my life without my older sister. I felt as if I had been suddenly dropped into the middle of a hurricane that came out of nowhere. This storm had engulfed me until seeing and breathing were difficult. No one around me could truly answer any of my questions or help me make sense of what had happened because they too were consumed with their own grief. For some unknown reason, I did not want to ask for help for fear of throwing off the fragile family balance.

A friend once told me that your older sibling encompasses all aspects of your life—your past, present, and future. When one of your older siblings dies, it's especially difficult because he or she is connected to your childhood memories, your present life, and your future life. You think your brother or sister is going to walk through your life journey with you, from beginning to end, or close to it. When my sister died, my carefree, self-indulgent teenage world ended abruptly. My life was never going to be the same, of this I was certain. The rest of my senior year passed by in a fog with lots of tears and many days of just going through the motions.

But like waves of the ocean that continue cresting and falling, each moment in time continues on—whether we want it to or not. As hard as we tried, we just could not turn back the hands of time and bring Mary K back, nor could we stop time from moving on without her. As C.S. Lewis said in his book *A Grief Observed*, "All that is gone. It is part of the past. And the past is the past and that is what time means, and time itself is one more name for death, and Heaven itself is a state where the former things have passed away." My plans for the future, moving away to attend college and going out into the world, forever changed. I knew in my heart that my parents needed me close, needed me home to support them through their grief. I decided to go to community college and live at home. Our family would never be the same and neither would the life I had envisioned for myself beyond high school. Little did I know, this was just the beginning.

2

TIME MARCHES ON— WHETHER WE WANT IT TO OR NOT!

The lives of all people flow through time, and, regardless of how brutal one moment may be, how filled with grief or pain or fear, time flows through all lives equally.

—Orson Scott Card

In the spring after my sister died, I was shopping with some girlfriends when I came across a framed picture of the famous poem "Footprints," by Mary Stevenson. The poem was framed in purple, my sister's favorite color, with a butterfly at the bottom of the poem. As I was standing there looking at this framed poem, I felt a force nudging me to buy it. I was really missing my sister, and this poem gave me immense comfort. It also matched perfectly with a cross-stitch that my sister had made for me the Christmas before she died. The cross-stitch read:

> *Memories of childhood we share and treasure. A special*
> *friendship one cannot measure. A love that is always*
> *deep and true. These are my feelings, my Sister, for you.*

Little did I know at the time, there would be great symbolism and future meaning to the butterfly at the bottom of the "Footprints" poem.

When faced with an out-of-order death, so sudden and unexpected, it is difficult to know where to begin. My parents eventually did the best they could to help my brother and me work through our grief. Looking back on it now, I can see that my dad threw himself into his work in order to cope; my mom focused on helping to care for my sister's baby; and my brother, being much like my dad, worked at being a good business partner for my dad. I lived at home while attending a local community college, worked part time, and tried to help my parents out when I could. We missed and grieved for my sister, each in our own individual way. We did not talk about her much, but there was a constant reminder of her absence in our everyday lives. One constant reminder was evident in my brother's averted eyes when he would notice my mom or me crying at a family meal or gathering. There was just no escaping the void left in our family.

Dealing with the death of my sister continued to be a constant battle; I thought about her and missed her every day. I still felt cheated, as I never got to have an adult sister relationship, especially after I became the mother of three kids of my own. But with the passage of time, the birth of my children, and the business of life, it became bearable. I learned to accept her absence and began filling it in by focusing on my teaching job, my children, and finding a new normal for my life. Our family did the best we could, as families do, to put the shattered pieces of our hearts together. We tried to find happiness and meaning in our lives without my sister. As time marched, on we lived with the constant worry we were going to forget some of the precious memories we shared as a family. Memories of the childhood I shared with my sister were always going to be cherished memories of a past, but not of a present.

After my sister's death in 1986, I started and finished college, got married, and had three beautiful children. Named after my sister, my first born child, Mary K Elizabeth Butt, was born in October 1994. David was born next, in 1997, and finally Jeremy in 2000. Having three children in six years, plus working full time kept me extremely busy, but not too busy to ponder how different my life would have been had I still had an older sister with whom to share my parenting experiences. I longed for that adult sibling relationship I felt so robbed and cheated from having. I was haunted with the never-ending *what could have*, or more accurately, *what should have been* for me in adulthood.

Sixteen years after my sister's death, my daughter, Mary, was in second grade. She was a very typical oldest child with two younger brothers to help care for and pester. Mary loved taking care of her brothers, always helping. She really enjoyed being around people and was an extremely busy child. She sang in the church choir, played in the church bell choir, and played soccer and baseball. She also loved art and drawing; she actually was quite a gifted artist for an eight year old. She was one of those kids who always had a smile on her face and was the life of every holiday and birthday party.

My middle child, David, was in kindergarten. He relied heavily on his older sister to be his fearless leader. Mary helped make sure he was on the right bus and even checked in with his teacher when she heard a boy in David's class was being mean to him. He was very comfortable allowing Mary to take the lead in most of their sibling adventures. David played on a T-ball team, was quiet and easygoing, and had—and still has—a sweet, tender way about him.

Jeremy was three years old, and his main goal in life was to get into his older siblings' toys and create havoc. He was busy, into everything, as three year olds tend to be. Jeremy looked up to David and Mary and looked to them to lead the way. Mary loved to dote on Jeremy and often tried to mother him, sometimes much to his annoyance. Between the three kids, Jeremy was at the age that kept me the busiest. I also made great efforts to make sure my children spent time with my nephew, my sister's only child. He was now seventeen years old, and in spite of the age gap with my children, he enjoyed spending time with them.

Time had indeed continued on after my sister's death, and, in spite of how painful and difficult it had been, we had learned to go on with our lives. We had forged a new path in her absence, but there was still a void that would never be filled. Time does heal in some ways, but never completely. We learned to accept what was beyond our control. At this point in my life in my grief over my sister's death, I had come to believe my family had paid our dues, suffered our loss. God would not allow another tragedy to befall our family. Oh, how wrong I was! The year 2003 would be another year that would change our lives irrevocably.

3

JUST ANOTHER DAY ... OR NOT?

There are things that happen in a person's life that are so scorched in the memory and burned into the heart, that there's no forgetting them.

—John Boyne

It was the first warm day of spring, Saturday, May 3, 2003. We had a busy day planned. Mary was going to play in her first baseball game. She was excited and eager for the day to begin. The three kids, my husband, and I piled into our van to meet the kids' grandparents for a late breakfast. We went back to the grandparents' house to wait until the game started. Mary drew a picture of a tiger in the jungle while we waited.

Mary's first game was a huge success. She played second base, hit the ball every time she was up to bat, and overall had a great time playing with her friends and teammates. We headed home after the game, as I was supposed to have a planning meeting at the house for Bible school. My sister-in-law and her kids came over, and we started working on our Bible school planning. As the cousins went outside to play tag in the yard, Mary's dad was just finishing mowing.

Suddenly my niece Katie, Mary's best friend since the girls were born, came running into the house yelling, "Aunt Barb you need to call 911; Mary has fallen, and she isn't getting up!" From this moment forward, it was as if my life was put into slow motion. I made the call, not having any idea how serious the situation outside was. I put the phone down and ran outside to investigate so I could tell the 911 operator what was wrong. Mary had collapsed, wasn't breathing. All I remember thinking was, *Not my Mary, not Mary, please, God, not Mary.* How was this happening? A perfectly healthy eight-year-old child just collapses while playing tag with her cousins in the front yard. This wasn't possible.

Oh, but it was.

My sister-in-law tried giving Mary CPR. I sent my son David over to see if our neighbor, a nurse, was home; the squad came; they worked on Mary; the helicopter came, and off she went to Children's

Hospital, her dad in the helicopter with her. We frantically drove to Children's, clinging to the hope of a miracle, praying the entire way, *God, please, not Mary, she's only eight, and she is so full of life.* I knew as soon as we walked into the ER. I could tell by the look on the nurse's face that my precious Mary was gone. I had to be living in a nightmare, floating in some foreign world. How could this be happening? Just an hour ago she was perfectly healthy; she even played her first ball game four hours before. This doesn't happen, right? Parents are not supposed to outlive their children; this is not the order that life is supposed to follow; and, yet, this has now happened twice in my family.

We were quickly ushered into the trauma area in the back. I saw Mary in a room off to the side, silent, inert, dead—just like that, gone. All her grandparents were there. The ER gave us time to say goodbye. Everyone took time to hug Mary. My mind couldn't comprehend what was happening. Say goodbye? This cannot be reality. I was given a phone by one of the nurses; they needed a decision right then about donating Mary's organs. I said yes, but later found out that it was too late; she had actually died at the house. Sadly, too much time had passed to use any of her organs.

This might sound strange, but I wanted out of there. I knew her body was there, but my heart could not feel her presence, and the pain was just too overwhelming. I wanted to run out of the hospital screaming at the top of my lungs. If I could get away, I would not have to face the grim reality staring me in the face: my daughter, gone, gone forever. Never again to see those sparkling, bright brown eyes staring back at me; never again to hear her infectious laugh; never again to revel in that beautiful, radiant smile of hers. The heartache was suffocating me. Run! Run! Run!

I began journaling almost immediately after Mary's death, continuing off and on for almost four years. Now, going back and reading the journal almost twelve years later, I relive my raw emotions from that time. The newness was so deep, cuttingly painful; I still cry when I read it.

> *May 5, 2003, two days after Mary's death: I must get out of bed, shower, get dressed. I must eat. I must pay attention to David and Jeremy, to be there for them during this difficult time. I must make decisions about how to honor your wonderful life so that everyone can know how special you were. Everyone who knew you knows how special you were, but I want them to remember you always.*

> *May 22, 2003, nineteen days after Mary's death: This is a sad day for me. I am remembering where I was when I heard the news. The first thing I did was panic. I thought I was calling 911 because you fell and broke a bone. When I went outside and realized how serious it was, I could not understand how you could be playing one minute and happy with life, and then be just lying there on the ground not breathing. It was very surreal. I felt like my world was standing still and that what was happening just could not be possible.*

> *Undated journal entry shortly after Mary died: Watching you go was agonizing and made me feel so helpless. It was the hardest thing I have ever done. I wasn't ready for you to be snatched away from our*

family. Death is so very cold; I wish I could get the
image out of my mind of you in the ER at Children's.
I want to remember your smiling face and you full of
life.

Reading these journal entries, you might begin to feel my pain, my agony, my shock, and sense my deep heartbreak and utter disbelief. Those of you who have gone through this kind of sudden loss can sadly and most certainly relate. Just getting out of bed is a challenge.

In the week that followed Mary's death, I have some very vivid memories, yet, in some respects, it was all just a blur. Decisions had to be made. Somehow we managed to get through the calling hours, the memorial service, and the burial. Hundreds of family and friends poured through our house, cooked, cleaned, organized, brought meals, and were just there to support us. There were notes and cards that included stories about Mary that we will always treasure. I am so thankful for the amount of love shown to us by our friends, family, and our church family. It seemed that every person in our church and our small community beyond the church reached out to us in some special way.

One vivid memory I do have the week after Mary died involves my brother. To know my brother is to love him. He has one of the most giving, tender hearts of anyone I know. What he did for me the week after Mary's death is a gift I could never repay. Mary died on a Saturday, and her funeral wasn't until the following Thursday. My brother refused to leave my house. He stayed with me every night after Mary died until after the memorial service. He literally slept in the recliner for five nights straight and did not go home. The time he took to be there for me is something I will never forget. Oh, how I love him for being there for me during my darkest hours. It reminded me of how we supported each other throughout the night of my sister's calling hours. If it were not for him and the support of so many others, I do not know how I would have made it.

We held Mary's memorial service in the gymnasium at her elementary school because we needed a place to accommodate hundreds of people. Mary loved school and learning, so having her final goodbye there seemed very fitting.

May 10, 2003, written two days after her memorial service: It was a beautiful sunny day. It rained the day before and after, but not on the day of your memorial service. There were balloons and flowers everywhere. I laughed when I saw the papier-mâché cow from the art show you had been telling me so much about. The service was an awesome tribute for an awesome little girl.

I see hope in this entry. In spite of the intense sadness that gripped my soul, I was able to write about what I knew Mary would have loved: balloons, flowers, the cow, and the sunny day.

Once people started back to their everyday lives, the real work began for us. Going from a happy family of five to a shattered family of four was quite the cross to bear. The next step for me was not only to figure out how to help myself and my two other children handle this overwhelming grief, it was also to find answers. I wanted definitive answers about why Mary died, and I was determined to know, without a doubt, that this was not going to happen to my remaining children. Thus began the longest, darkest, loneliest journey of my entire life. Finding the answer to the question, why two Marys had died so suddenly and both so young, haunted me. I refused to rest until I had all my questions answered.

4

I WANT ANSWERS!

Life is filled with unanswered questions, but it is the courage to seek those answers that continues to give meaning to life. You can spend your life wallowing in despair, wondering why you were the one who was led towards the road strewn with pain, or you can be grateful that you are strong enough to survive it.

—J.D. Stroube

When your world is shaken to its very core, like mine was, some of us want to bury our heads in the sand and wish it all away. Initially, I wanted to do that, but more than anything I wanted to find out why Mary died. The haunting question gnawed at me nonstop. How could a perfectly healthy eight-year-old child collapse and die while playing tag in the front yard? This is not normal; it is freakish; I did not know a single person who had a child die this way. I had to know *why*. I had to make sure without a doubt that it was not something I had done wrong, or, even worse, it was not something that could happen again to my remaining children, then six and three years old. I vividly recall having a conversation with one of the doctors who performed Mary's autopsy at Children's a few days after her death. I explained to him that my sister had died very suddenly, also very young, in almost exactly the same way in 1986. Could these deaths be related? His response to me was simple; there was no correlation between their deaths; it was just a strange coincidence. At the time I believed what he said. After all, he was a doctor; he should know. Wrong! Oh, so wrong!

The preliminary autopsy reports showed that Mary died from brain stem herniation. Doctors believed it was caused by a cyst the size of a pea found on her pineal gland, the core center of the brain. Supposedly, she was born with it. I began researching and trying to understand everything I could find about cysts on the brain. I read books about brain tumors. I called the Brain Tumor Foundation in Washington, DC, to learn more. I scheduled appointments for my two children to have a magnetic resonance imaging test (MRI)— just to be sure they didn't have something like this as well. I was determined to have my remaining children checked from head to toe; I was going to leave no stone unturned. After all, Mary had appeared healthy, and look what had happened to her. Fear was hanging on the wall in every room of my house, terrorizing me, fear that yet another tragedy was lurking; fear clung to every fiber of my being; I just could not take the chance that my boys were born with the same cyst.

Mary died at the beginning of May. As we were having MRIs near the end of July, I was explaining to the doctor the reason for testing the boys. He listened intently to my motherly plea. *Please make sure my kids don't die like Mary did.* His response to me is one I will never forget. "The cyst they found on your daughter's brain did not cause her death. There is no way a cyst the size of a pea could have caused her to die." The room began to spin; I thought I was going to pass out. To say I had a complete meltdown would have been an understatement. So, according to this doctor, what I thought for the last three months had been the cause of Mary's death was not at all accurate. Did I hear him correctly? He repeated it for me. Yes, he had indeed told me exactly what I thought I had heard him say. Back to square one: disbelief, shock, anger, gut-wrenching agony. The rug was pulled out from under me again, just as I was regaining my footing.

At this point I decided I would become more aggressive, more assertive. I called the office of the top neurosurgeon at Children's Hospital, explained my situation, and pleaded with him to schedule an appointment for me. An expert on brain tumors, he would have to know without a doubt if this cyst caused Mary's death or not. The receptionist must have taken pity on me because she went ahead and scheduled an appointment. With a copy of the autopsy in hand, I marched into the neurosurgeon's office hoping I would find the answers I was so desperately seeking. I explained the situation, and he looked over Mary's autopsy. His response was the same as the doctor who performed the MRI on my boys; the cyst could not have caused her death. *So what did?*

Since Mary's autopsy was performed at Children's and he was a doctor who also worked there, he told me he would set up a meeting for all the doctors involved in her autopsy, including himself, to discuss her case. I will forever be indebted to this man, who most likely will never realize the enormity of what he did for me. Organizing this type of meeting takes time, and it was nearly five weeks before he was able to get the meeting scheduled and call me with the results of their discussion. All the doctors involved knew the family history of two sudden deaths at a young age. Two doctors stood behind the pineal gland cyst cause of death; another doctor made a very profound statement in the meeting. He thought it had to be something heart-related. He said that if he were a member of this family, he would run, not walk, to the nearest cardiologist and get checked. The results of the meeting were inconclusive. The comment by the doctor about the heart theory was my ray of hope, the one lead I had been searching for in this journey to find answers. Thus began an entirely new direction of investigation; something heart-related could have caused Mary's death.

It was now the beginning of November, nearly six months since Mary had died. I began searching sudden death and heart-related deaths for young people on the Internet. I had some questions about the information I found, so I called a girlfriend in South Carolina whose husband was a cardiologist in order to learn more about causes of heart-related deaths. He, too, felt Mary's death was heart-related. One day as I was searching the Internet, I stumbled upon a website that was all about unexplained sudden death in young people. It had stories about families where people had died just like Mary, young, healthy, no apparent reason or cause. One particular story caused me to stop dead in my tracks. It was a story about a girl who had died very young. Diagnosed with epilepsy, she had had a couple of episodes where she fainted while swimming and almost drowned. My sister? She, too, had almost drowned twice while we were growing up and also had been diagnosed with epilepsy. The girl I was reading about had died from a heart condition called Long QT Syndrome (Long QTS), and as I read, I discovered this was a genetic heart condition. My blood ran cold. My stomach went instantly into knots. This had to be the answer I had been searching for. It just had to be. My entire family needed to be tested, *now*.

I called my brother and his wife and my parents. I explained my theory, and they agreed it was worth checking into. My brother's kids were the first to have an electrocardiogram (EKG). My sister-in-law called me as they left the cardiologist; her kids, my niece and nephew, both tested positive for Long QTS. A wave of emotions washed over me: shock, disbelief, joy, sorrow, and, yet, a great sense of relief. When it was all said and done, in addition to my niece and nephew, my brother, father, and I all had Long QTS. Both of my boys tested negative, as did my sister's son. The answer I had been searching for was finally here. We knew without a doubt that both my sister and my daughter had died from this genetic heart condition. Talk about bittersweet. They died so we could live. Sadly profound.

This answer-finding saga took me almost seven months. Many well-meaning friends and family along the way thought I was losing my mind, that I was too obsessed with wanting to know why Mary died.

Put this behind you.

Just move on.

Just let it go; let it go.

It doesn't matter why Mary died; when I wake up tomorrow she will still be dead.

You need to focus your time and energy on your boys.

Though many worried I had gone off the deep end—and I often wondered if they were right—I knew deep down there had to be some logical explanation that would help me understand what had happened and help me find peace. Finding the answer to why Mary died became my healing journey, my lifeline to hold onto. Had I listened to my critics, I might have missed one of the most important journeys of my life.

My inner voice was the gut feeling that had fueled me on this quest to find the much-needed answers about my daughter's death. I believe I was hardwired with this gut feeling during this very dark time of my life. It came from deep within my heart and soul, but it was up to me to listen and take action. Often when God uses our inner voice to nudge us in the direction we need to go, we are not even aware He is at work. At the time, I did not realize God was encouraging me along this path; it wasn't until long after Mary's death that this became clear. I finally had the answers I so yearned for because I had listened to that inner voice. Even if people along your journey do not fully support you, even if they chastise you, even if you are beginning to question if they are right, listen to your gut feeling. Persevere!

5

LONG Q WHAT?

The difficulties in life are intended to make you better, not bitter.

—John C. Maxwell

Once we were all diagnosed with Long QT Syndrome, we began the medical process of learning about the treatment for this heart condition. My brother and I were put on the heart medication beta blockers right away. I had a reaction to the beta blockers and ended up in the hospital. The best course of treatment for my dad, brother, and me was to have an internal cardiac defibrillator (ICD) implanted. Doctors refused to let me leave until I had my surgery. I was so angry that the hospital would not let me go home, I almost walked out. I had two children who needed me, and once I was off the beta blockers I felt perfectly fine. At this point, I did not fully understand Long QTS, and I was just plain mad at the world in general. A very close friend talked me off the ledge and convinced me to stay in the hospital until the operation could be done.

In November 2003, I underwent surgery for my ICD; my dad had his surgery in December; my brother's surgery was in January. Katie and Joe, my niece and nephew, were too young to have an ICD implanted, so they were both put on beta blockers.

So what exactly is Long QT Syndrome? It is a disorder of the heart's electrical activity. The electrical system of the heart is fueled by the flow of tiny, electrically charged ions of sodium, calcium, potassium, and chloride, which move in and out of the cells of the heart. The QT interval is basically the section of the EKG which represents the time it takes for the electrical system of the heart to fire an impulse through the ventricles and then recharge. Simply stated, the QT interval is the time it takes for the heart muscle to contract and then recover. This is measured in milliseconds on an EKG. In congenital Long QTS, one of these ion channels is blocked, so the electrical signal has to find a different route to travel. This is the reason the heart resting rate between beats is longer.

Long QTS is a rhythm disorder that can potentially cause fast, chaotic heartbeats. These rapid heartbeats have three possible results; they can trigger a fainting spell and you wake up; you can faint and have a seizure; or in some rare cases, you can faint and not wake up, which results in sudden death. Long QT Syndrome occurs in one in every two thousand to five thousand people. Two triggers for Long QTS can be swimming and exercise. With a Long QT event, the electrical system of the heart is not working properly, so the heart beats with an abnormal rhythm. When a normal person exercises, runs, or swims, the heart rate increases and the pause between beats shortens. With a person who has Long QTS, the heart rate also increases, but the pause between beats lengthens. The longer pause is caused by one of the electrical ion channels of the heart's signal being blocked. When the QT interval is longer than normal, it increases the risk for *torsade de pointes,* a life-threatening form of ventricular tachycardia or rapid heartbeat. This is the genetic error or mistake that makes up Long QTS.

Sudden death is extremely rare, especially as the first symptom or event. My sister had symptoms, but Long QTS was very difficult to diagnose in the 1980s, since it was a newly discovered genetic heart condition. My mom remembers my sister coming home from basketball conditioning in high school and saying that the running made her feel light-headed and dizzy, so she decided not to try out for the team. The age when a person is most at risk for symptoms from Long QTS range from eight to twenty, but it is possible to have an event at any age. My daughter's first symptom at age eight was, tragically, sudden death.

There are seven known types of Long QTS, and more are being discovered each year. Type 1, 2, and 3 are the most common. Long

QT 1 has symptoms triggered by exercise and swimming; Long QT 2 has symptoms trigged by a loud noise or by startling the person; Long QT 3 is the type where events occur when the person is asleep. Extensive research has been done about connecting SIDS to Long QT 3. Most often, multiple triggers are needed in order to induce a fainting spell, a seizure, or, in the worst case, sudden death.

Finding and diagnosing Long QTS is not easy. For some families, mine included, it is like finding a needle in a haystack. A cardiologist really has to be looking for it. They also need to know the family history and have extensive knowledge about this particular heart condition in order to properly diagnose it. Once we knew about this genetic heart condition, I pulled all the available medical records for everyone in my family. Ironically, I discovered that my paternal grandfather had had an EKG right before he died in 1994, and this test clearly showed a prolonged QT interval. Sadly, knowing the family history is imperative in properly diagnosing this condition, none of his doctors forewarned us of this finding. All the adults, including cousins, aunts, and uncles, needed to be tested with an EKG. We were immediately placed under the care of a cardiologist who specialized in Long QT Syndrome.

For my family, this meant some drastic changes. Each adult with Long QTS learned to live with an internal cardiac device almost immediately after his/her diagnosis. My niece, once she turned sixteen, also had an ICD implanted. My nephew, age seventeen, is still on beta blockers. Team sports that entailed a lot of exercise and running were no longer an option for my niece and nephew. Swimming was also on the restricted list, but this has more recently been lifted and my nephew is now able to swim with supervision and an on-site automated external defibrillator (AED). As with any medical condition, Long QTS is in a state of constant flux because of research, and the doctors are forever adjusting treatment based on newly learned information.

After our surgeries, I spent many hours researching and learning more about this genetic heart condition. To finally have the answers I had been diligently searching for was an overwhelming relief, but it also brought on some new and unexpected emotions. One that was most prevalent was survivor's guilt. How is it possible that I was able to save myself and other members of my family, but I still couldn't save the one person I so wanted to save? Here is a journal entry I wrote right after we learned about the Long QTS diagnosis.

November 2003 six months after Mary died: I finally found out what happened to cause your death, and how I wish we could have stumbled onto this sooner. You continue to touch people beyond what we could have even imagined. I feel good about helping so many with this discovery but feel let down that I couldn't help the girl I wanted to the most.

June 15, 2004 over a year after Mary died: These are the days when I want to turn back time, before we knew about Long QTS and had all the restrictions for Katie and Joe. I feel so bad that they have to change their lives because of what I've discovered. I know I should feel good about us now knowing, but I feel bad that they cannot do what most kids their age get to do.

A year after we were diagnosed with Long QTS, my sister-in-law, mother, and I flew out to Salt Lake City, Utah, to attend a conference that focused on heart conditions like Long QTS. I was able to meet the doctor who discovered this genetic heart condition and many of the top experts of Long QTS. It was at that point I felt a sense of peace in this search I had been on for answers. I was no longer driven to know, driven to find out; I felt a great sense of resolution at that point. The inner drive had finally spent itself out. I could stop focusing on the why of both Marys' deaths and begin focusing on learning to live a new life without my daughter.

6

AND THE FOG DESCENDED

Yesterday is gone. Tomorrow has not come. We have only today, Let us begin.

—Mother Teresa

June 23, 2003, seven weeks after Mary died: When I heard you were gone I felt my heart shatter to pieces and a part of me died with you. I've had a pit in my stomach ever since that terrible day. Every time I eat, my stomach turns to knots. My life feels like part of me is missing, and all I want is to have that part back. I feel overwhelmed with sadness. I felt my comfortable and solid world crumble apart, as I cannot grasp that you are really gone. I don't know how I am going to live without you. You were such a bright spot in my day. You brought a spark and light to our family that can never be replaced.

The thing about grief is that you cannot get around it; you have to go through it. Thirteen years after my daughter's death and thirty years after my sister's death, I am still grieving. There are numerous technical, clinical books about the stages of grief and how to work through the grief process. I tried reading them after Mary died but just didn't have the attention span or the energy to comprehend the scientific terminology about grief. My brain was in slow motion when it came to processing information involving deep thought. I did find books written by people who had shared a similar experience much more heartfelt and, overall, more helpful. These books, written by the people who had really been through it, conveyed comfort and pearls of wisdom I could understand and relate to. Knowing that others had survived loss and deep grief offered me hope that I could also overcome the great obstacles before me.

Often people say time heals all wounds, but I only agree with this to a point. Some wounds never completely heal. The wounds left by losing a loved one might indeed heal, but they can suddenly break open at any time, even decades later. People talk about having closure with grief, and with this I disagree. Closure refers to leaving something behind and moving on. It is true that life goes on whether we want it to or not, but I think acceptance is a more accurate term than closure—accepting that you cannot change the past, accepting the fact that life just isn't fair, accepting what is beyond your control. Acceptance is an important key in the grief healing process. Our hearts can only be healed with the help of faith, sometimes blind faith. This healing and acceptance takes time, years of time, so we must be gentle and patient with ourselves.

May 22, 2003, written nineteen days after Mary's death: The hardest thing for me today is that I am at work and am crying inside because I miss you so much. I want to hug you, tell you I love you, braid your hair, clean your usually smudged glasses, lay out your clothes, I just want you near me. I miss kissing you on the head and hugging you close.

October 4, 2003, five months after Mary died: I feel like screaming. I hate hurting so much and feeling so sad. I used to look forward to weekends so much, and now they are so hard. It is hard to enjoy anything right now. My heart is so heavy. I am very tired. I do not want to have your birthday without your smiling face.

October 9, 2003: I wonder if there will ever be a day I don't feel like I got socked in the gut every time I think about you. I should be planning your ninth birthday party, and that makes me angry and sad all at once.

October 25, 2003: Right now I would like to shut myself in your room and hide from the world. I feel as if I could cry for days and never run out of tears. I never knew my body could hurt so much and endure such sadness. I wonder if there will ever be a day when my body doesn't ache from missing you so much. It is so difficult not to get sucked into the darkness of sadness and forget about living altogether.

Clearly these journal entries were very early in my grief process. Whenever I reread my journal, I can feel the immense pain in the words. A quote by C.S Lewis comes to mind when I read this last journal entry: "I not only live each endless day in grief, but live each day thinking about living each day in grief." Oh, how true this quote is, especially when experiencing the early stages of grief. Grief absolutely consumes every waking moment.

I have a unique perspective on grief in that I have lost a sibling and a child. When an out-of-order death occurs, one thing is certain, you will never be the same person again. The deaths of my sister and daughter were devastating, but in very different ways. Losing my sister gave me an idea of the kind of loss my own children have experienced with the death of their own big sister. I tried to make sure they had opportunities to express their sorrow through counseling and attending grief day camp the summer after Mary died. Helping my boys through their grief and dealing with the weight of my own grief was overwhelming, to say the least.

October 18, 2003: David asked me tonight if I thought Santa might bring us a new Mary. This made me sad to my very core. I know he is missing her so much, I just wish I could help him more. We all miss Mary so much, it is hard to put into words. Jeremy said something today about when Mary gets better she'll play in the tent they made. This is all so very hard. I pray for strength every day.

January 16, 2004: Jeremy keeps telling me not to worry, that we're going to get a new Mary. He just doesn't understand that this isn't going to change the fact that Mary is gone. I want so much to feel better when we're all together; it is just hard to do anything as a family when such a lively part of it is missing. Her brothers really looked up to her and relied on her for guidance.

I vividly recall David asking me one day, "Why can't we just dig Mary up and keep her?" This question took my breath away. I then tried to proceed with an explanation a child could understand about why we could no longer keep his sister. My children were very young at the time of their sister's death, and it was clearly very difficult for them to understand the finality of death and that their beloved sister was never coming home again.

Experiencing a sudden death is like being thrust into prison where the walls of grief, anger, guilt, emptiness, denial, and sadness can close in on you quickly. Nelson Mandela spent twenty-seven years in prison surviving long bouts of solitary confinement. He was even kept from attending his own son's funeral. During his years in prison he often took comfort in reciting a poem to fellow inmates. The poem he recited is titled "Invictus," by William Ernest Henley. The last stanza of the poem reads;

> *It matters not how strait the gate,*
> *How charged with punishments the scroll,*
> *I am the master of my fate,*
> *I am the captain of my soul.*

It can be difficult to find comfort in your darkest hours. Find something like this poem that offers you comfort and hope, something that carries you through your darkest times. Focus on it. Recite it aloud. Share it with a friend. Use it as a lifeline to avoid being overcome and drowning in your grief. I have a wall of quotes in my closet that I began collecting when Mary died. It is an accumulation of Bible verses, inspirational quotes, and special greeting cards. This collage of quotes has inspired me over the years and helped to keep me focused on positive thoughts. It was the visual reminder, a lighthouse amidst the storms of grief. This wall of quotes has offered me hope on those days I so desperately needed uplifted when I was alone, feeling as if I could not face another day without my precious Mary and my older sister Mary K.

Grief can be like a whirlpool trying to suck you in, making you feel like you are about to drown. There are various ways we can work through grief, but understand that what works for some, may not work at all for others. Grief is exhausting work, but, unfortunately, it must be done. No, not overnight. To be honest, I am still working through my grief each and every day. Writing this book is just another way of processing my own grief, but my overall hope is that it gives you comfort. Each day brings on its own challenges, and when grief is fresh and new, making it through the day can be an amazing feat all its own. I remember how I wanted to put on the brakes of time and not move forward after Mary died. One has to make a conscious decision to live life and not stand still while life continues on around you. Working through grief is key in rediscovering yourself and getting life back on track, or as on track as possible.

The week following my daughter Mary's death was grueling. There was so much going on—a constant flow of people in and out of our house, the phone ringing nonstop, important decisions that had to be made, meeting with the funeral home to arrange her funeral and pick out a casket, interviews by the reporters from the newspaper, interviews by the sheriff investigating her death, the memorial service to plan; the list was endless. I think I went into autopilot mode, yet I also vividly recall a feeling that came over me that Mary needed me to be strong so I could pay tribute to her life. I remember taking people up on the many offers of help that week, from a friend going to pick up a dress for me to wear to the calling hours, to Mary's grandma going to pick out a dress for Mary to be buried in. I strongly urge you to lean on your friends and family during this time; allow them to do for you.

One poignant memory I have from that week is the night of the calling hours. Three very dear friends I worked with offered to stay at our house. Their plan was to clean our house while we were gone. I took them up on the offer, as I had done with so many other kind and generous ones throughout the week and would continue to do for weeks to come. As we were walking out the door to head to the church, I recall looking down and seeing the line of shoes by the door. Instantly, I told my friends, "Please do not move her shoes." I desperately needed that visual reminder of Mary. I was nowhere near ready to part with them so soon. I was holding onto her shoes by the door like a life jacket keeps one afloat in deep water.

I'm sharing this story about not moving Mary's shoes for two reasons. The first is to show that this was what I needed at that moment to help me work through my grief. Another person may have reacted completely opposite, finding her shoes by the door too painful a reminder. Each person's grief is unique and specific to them. What helps ease one person's pain may do just the opposite for another. Ironically, shoes are a metaphor for moving on, and I was not ready to move on at that point. The second reason is to share that, with the passage of time, I was able to move Mary's shoes. After nearly a month and a half, I decided it was time to pack her shoes away and give them to charity. Allowing me that time to adjust and work through my intense grief was a vitally important part of my healing.

The days and weeks after Mary's death, I recall feeling as if I were a prisoner of grief from which there was no escape. I was in a constant state of struggle between wanting so desperately to live in the past, and yet coping with the here and now. I struggled with the memories of my life before Mary died, and with the constant *what could have been* for her life and the life of my family. This question gnawed at me: *how do the ones left behind keep from drowning in the thoughts of all the life events we will never get to see our loved one do?* I blindly attempted to sort through this new normal rhythm of life, but for me, nothing would ever be normal again. As I attempted to navigate the minefield of grief, I battled an overwhelming sense of brokenness, guilt, loneliness, and never-ending tears. The passage of time was the only element that helped ease these intense and crippling feelings. I'd like to give you the gift of wisdom in this book, but that's something only the passing years can bring.

There are few guarantees in this world, but one of them is that all of us will face adversity in one way or another. We need to use our suffering to build character, not give into it, or allow it to destroy us. This is easier said than done. Finding outlets for our pain and suffering that can offer hope and peace is the key. Avoid unhealthy outlets that beget more suffering. Don't allow suffering in your life to perpetuate and rule you and keep you from finding your path through the darkness. Suffering can make you or break you. Only you can decide which one it will be for you.

> *September 28, 2003*: *We went to a fundraiser last night that was held in your memory. It was just awesome. Organizers sold T-shirts with your picture on them. There was a silent auction and a live auction that raised almost $10,000 to help the Second Chance Humane Society. They are going to build "Mary's Place," which I know would make you smile. You were such an animal lover. You would say you were glad to see us all laughing and glad we had an event in your memory. You would tell me that you were proud or glad we had an event that was so much fun to honor and remember you.*

> *May 9, 2004, a year after Mary died: We had a walk in your memory on Sunday, May 2, 2004. Over six hundred people came and we raised over $12,000 to pay for AEDs in the local schools. We are also sending some money to the SADS Foundation. The weather*

was terrible. It was cold and rainy, but the day was a great success. I did a short speech about things we remembered about you. At many points during the day I thought how much you'd love the walk. All the family and friends who knew and loved you were there. There were also people at the walk who had never met you. The overwhelming support was a great reflection of how many people loved you. Oh, how we miss you and wish you were here.

You can clearly tell from these journal entries that, when I wrote about doing something positive with my grief, there was hope. These journal entries are very different from the ones I shared earlier. Grieving is work, a continual process, exhausting and difficult, but it must be done in order to heal. As the introductory quote states, *We only have today, let us begin.* If we can focus on taking it one day at a time, sometimes even one hour at a time, our healing journey can take place.

7

AND THE POT BOILS OVER

Don't hold on to anger, hurt or pain. They steal your energy and keep you from love.

—Leo Buscaglia

At the beginning of processing the untimely death of a loved one, it takes some time to emerge from the dense fog before the anger sets in; at least it did for me. Anger is a very normal emotion experienced after unexpected death. You are bound to feel cheated out of time you didn't get to spend, memories you didn't get to create with the one you lost. It is especially hard not to focus on all the future moments lost when a loved one dies young. It would be difficult not to feel anger at one point or another. After my sister and daughter died, I had many moments of intense anger. Some produced positive results, and some did not.

A few months after my sister died, I remember being angry with my friends one day at lunch for talking about what I perceived as trivial, unimportant high school stuff. I vividly remember getting up from the lunch table and storming out, thinking to myself, *How could they talk about something so unimportant?* All I wanted to talk about was the wave of intense grief and sadness that had descended upon my heart and life. I did not have the energy to think about the lives of my friends, whose daily routines were still intact and unchanged. I was jealous of them, angry that nothing had changed for them when everything in my world had been turned completely upside down.

After my daughter Mary died, the list of targets for my anger was endless. I was angry with the doctors for not helping me figure out why Mary died; I was angry at myself for not being a better mother and preventing her death; I was angry about the newspaper article that reported her death as *under investigation*; I was angry at everyone who got to tuck in all their children every night while I did not; I was angry that I had a genetic heart condition that had so drastically changed my own life; and, yes, I was angry at God for allowing this to happen, not once, but now twice in my family. Everything that I was angry about was beyond my control, which is probably what made me the angriest. Facing the litany of ideals I once had naively thought I actually had control over in my life was difficult, to say the least.

> *July 18, 2003, two and a half months after Mary died:*
> *Dear Mary, I am so angry and frustrated with so many*
> *things right now. I am angry that I have to continue*
> *living my life without you. I do not understand why, if*
> *the cyst you had was so rare, why you had to have one.*
> *I am angry that I did not get to hug you and kiss you*
> *and tell you how much I love you before you left this*
> *world. I am angry that your brothers will have very*
> *little memory of you and how much you adored them. I*
> *hurt so much. I've tried so hard to be a good mom, and*
> *I feel like I've failed simply because I could not protect*
> *your brothers from such a traumatic experience. I am*
> *so mad that they have to go through such a sad and*
> *tragic event so young in their lives.*

Anger is seeping from the words in this journal entry.

Working through my feelings of anger continued to be a big part of the grief processing journey. I remember times when my anger consumed me, and I knew people around me could almost see the angry chip I had on my shoulder. It was extremely difficult to not get caught up in the anger connected to all the life milestones I knew I was going to miss out on. This journal entry expresses anger's hold on me.

I get really angry when I think we will never be able to see you graduate from high school and college. How I long to just enjoy seeing you grow into a young lady and get married, have children of your own, a career, etc. I know that whatever you had set your mind out to do, you would have done it well, as things came so easily for you. You were also such a hard worker from a very early age. I feel so very cheated when I dwell on all the milestones we won't ever get to share with you.

I mentioned earlier in this chapter that anger can also produce positive results. I can vividly recall the doctor at Children's Hospital, who was running tests on my boys, calmly telling me the cyst I had been told all along that caused Mary's death could not have been the cause at all. With this bit of news, I quickly went from disbelief and shock to intense anger, a pot boiling over. I was so angry at the doctors for misleading me and giving me false information about something so incredibly important. This anger fueled my inner fire; I immediately resolved not to rest until I had the definitive answer I so desperately searched for. In the midst of that intense anger toward the doctors, God was using me and my anger to follow the path He wanted me on. Finding the answers for the two unexplained young deaths in my family was God's pathway. My anger in that situation led to shockingly positive results.

May 8, 2007, four years after Mary died: I have not written in this journal in a long time. I guess I would like to tell God that I am sorry I've blamed Him, been angry with Him, and turned away from Him at times. Faith is such a hard concept to wrap my brain and

heart around. I feel like I've failed miserably at times.
I also feel like I've triumphed and overcome enormous
odds. I keep telling my heart to trust God's plan for me,
but it is just so hard. I tell my intellectual mind that
Mary is happy and living a full life in heaven, but my
heart just breaks and hurts still so. I'm just going to try
to do the best I can and have faith that it's all going to
be okay, and I'll see Mary in heaven someday.

My venting to God shows the intensity of the feelings of grief, but it also shows that I knew I needed to let go of my anger, trust God, and have faith in His plan for my life. In spite of the great sadness of missing my daughter and my sister, I used these tragedies and turned them into something positive. Do I wish there could have been another way around it, an easier way? Absolutely! Unfortunately, we are not given any choice in the life experiences we are faced with. We live in an imperfect world, and suffering and loss are bound to happen to all of us. Fortunately, we do have a choice in the way we play the cards of life that we are dealt.

8

THE WEIGHT OF THE WORLD

Guilt isn't always a rational thing. Guilt is a weight that will crush you whether you deserve it or not.

—Maureen Johnson

Guilt can manifest into a completely irrational way of thinking. Guilt is one of the most destructive emotions, especially when we are feeling guilty for events we have absolutely no control over. Guilt and time are closely connected. It can be a way of dragging the past into the future and avoiding the sometimes harsh reality of the present. Feelings of guilt are like carrying around a backpack full of bricks. Guilt can weigh us down to the point of utter defeat. Sadly, guilt surreptitiously infiltrates our hearts and minds, conscious and subconscious after a traumatic event or an extreme loss, in our darkest hours. Nonetheless, guilt is another unfortunate chapter in the unfolding saga of grief.

Webster's definition of guilt is: a bad feeling caused by knowing or thinking that you have done something bad or wrong. I think guilt can be way of holding us back from true healing. Guilt can grip you so tightly that you feel as if you are suffocating in its grasp.

> *Undated journal entry: I feel guilty because I've told so many people how much work having three kids is. I felt overwhelmed at the idea of having three children. In the back of my mind, I wonder if God took you because I said having three kids was too much for me to juggle. I feel guilty because I was not as patient with you as I should have been. I expected too much from you. I feel guilty about the last big fight we had about you not practicing piano enough. I feel guilty because I did not appreciate you more.*

All of these feelings of guilt are unfounded and destructive. At the time, my thoughts seemed logical, but looking back after many years have passed, it seems ridiculous that I would feel guilty about many untruths and unfounded ideas.

Mary's death was an event that just happened. My sister's death also just happened. There was no accident; no one was to blame; it was just the luck—or should I say the ill-luck—of the genetic draw. And, yet, I wrote frequently in my journal about this feeling of deep guilt over Mary's death. This wasn't even rational. When I read these journal entries now, I wonder how I could have been so irrational. Since guilt comes from the past, it is, at times, a way for us to keep the past alive.

During some of the time when I wrote a lot in my journal, I did not know why Mary had died.

> *May 18, 2003: When I let go, I feel scared that I cannot regain my composure. It is hard for me to let go because I worry that David and Jeremy will be scared and more traumatized. I also feel a bit of relief when I surrender. I need to let go of all my guilt about not being a good enough mom to you. You were such a special child; I want to rest easy knowing that you knew how much I loved you and that I appreciated so many things about you. I feel afraid of moving on with life without you. I want everything to stop, even go back, so that no one will forget how special you are.*

> *October 12, 2003: I feel like I failed as a mother. It is so hard to face the reality of how little control we have as parents. I, up to this point, had fooled myself into thinking I could do anything, get anything, or change anything. I now realize that this is forever false. It is*

so hard to trust myself right now, as I feel I failed you, Mary. The simple fact that there was and is nothing I can do to change the reality that you are gone is utterly unbearable. It is so hard to understand why a little girl who loved life, is no longer here to enjoy so many things. It is hard to trust that I am a good mother because of this intense feeling of failure. Please, God, help me feel like I didn't fail.

Clearly, the intense guilt I was feeling was breaking me down to the point that I didn't even see myself as a good mother. The simple fact that Mary's death was completely beyond my control did not even factor into my thinking. I could no more have prevented Mary's death than I could have stopped the sun from coming up, but I still allowed guilt to make me feel as if I had failed as a mother because I had not been able to prevent her death. Guilt was overriding common sense and good judgment. Deep in the trenches of grief, do not allow guilt to consume you.

October 3, 2004: Sometimes I feel guilty for not spending more time with you. I mean, we did a lot of things together, but if we'd known we were only going to have you with us for such a short time, we would have made more time to be together. Honestly, I don't think there is enough time to make up for the future we never get to spend with you.

Guilt serves no purpose other than to make you doubt yourself. Guilt does not play fair. Guilt plays tricks on the mind by making you believe something beyond your control is your fault. If you allow it to, guilt can eat away at your self-confidence and destroy you. When you dwell on guilt, you lose a little bit of yourself each day. Guilt seems to prey on you when you are at your weakest. Writing about my guilt in my journal was a way for me to release it, let go of it. Holding on to guilt is a way of self-destruction. I also prayed to God to take my guilt and set me free from it.

One last guilt-laden journal entry I wrote a little over three years after Mary died is about both my daughter and my sister:

> *How I wish my life were different. I feel guilty because I can remember less and less about my life when either Mary was alive. I guess you are supposed to focus your energy on living in the present? I just feel like I've lost touch with my daughter and my sister. I miss them both so terribly much. I feel like God has cheated me out of so much. I don't understand God's plan for my life, and I wonder if I ever will. I really wish God would post road signs up on the highway of life, giving me a sign or direction I should go to find a deeper meaning or purpose for my life.*

Even twenty years after my sister died, I was still feeling cheated and guilty for moving on with my life. We are supposed to move on with our lives. The difficult part of moving on is finding a way to include your lost loved one into your current life. Journaling about my guilt was a way for me to release myself from the grips of it. If journaling isn't for you, find another outlet for your guilt. Do not hold onto it, for it will only bring you down even further, and it will steal your chances of hope and happiness.

Anger and guilt are the dark and evil brothers in the grief process, but they are necessary emotions when processing intense grief. They can easily become like a thief in the night, robbing us of the much needed healing, happiness, and peace if we allow them. This robbing I am referring to occurs when we focus on or get stuck in anger or guilt. It happens when we hold onto it, cohabitating on an hourly or daily basis with these robbers called anger and guilt. Relinquishing what cannot be controlled, and asking God to help us accept what is, will put us on the right road to healing.

Guilt is a way of punishing ourselves, when in fact we need to forgive ourselves by letting go of the guilt. This is only possible when we fully understand we are loved by a greater power than ourselves, and He has already forgiven us. The key to healing from the damage done by guilt is forgiveness. Forgiveness means acknowledging the past and the events we have no control over and letting go. Do not allow your guilt to take away the life you have ahead of you. God is standing by, patiently waiting for us to release our guilt to Him.

9

THE NEVER-ENDING TUG-OF-WAR

The ultimate lesson all of us have to learn is unconditional love, which includes not only others but ourselves as well.

—Elisabeth Kübler-Ross

For years after Mary died, I found myself in a constant state of going back and forth. Early on, it was the going back and forth between holding on to my life that included Mary and the daunting task of moving on with my new life without her. Initially, I spent hours beating myself up thinking *if only* I had been a better mother or done this or that differently, *if only* I would have seen a warning sign, *if only* the doctor could have discovered her heart condition sooner. The list of *if onlys* was endless. A constant tug-of-war was going on in my mind and in my heart that, over time, wore me down into the depths of despair. My mind knew I needed to move on with my life for the sake of Mary's brothers and everyone else who loved and cared about me, but my heart was stuck between my life before Mary died and my new life now, without her.

Once I discovered the reason for Mary's death, the tug-of-war game went in an entirely different direction. I struggled with going from feeling grateful for discovering Long QTS for my family, to hating myself for being able to save my family and myself, but not Mary. On one hand, I was happy that we finally had answers and knew why Mary had died. On the other hand, I was so disappointed in myself because I could not save the one person I so desperately wanted to save. This was the supreme survivor's guilt phenomenon.

Several years after Mary died, a good friend pointed something out to me that was painful to admit at the time, but true. Basically, he said that I was holding on to my sadness as a way of holding onto Mary. His observation about me was spot on; I did feel that if I held onto the sadness of losing Mary, it was also a way to always keep her with me. This sadness was my last remnant, my remaining connection to keeping Mary with me. In reality, holding on to my sadness was my way of punishing myself for outliving my own daughter. Some of us feel we should be punished for being the one still living when our child, unfairly, has died. This is the out-of-order death I mentioned in an early chapter.

Over the years of working through my grief, the tug-of-war battles have remained constant and endless, although they have become less intense and consuming over time. It was the back and forth between denial and acceptance, between crying and laughing, between blaming myself and forgiving myself for something that was beyond my control, between feeling as if God were punishing me for not being a good enough mother to knowing God loves me in spite of my shortcomings, between the constant *if only I had done more* to knowing I had done everything within my power, between holding on to heartache and sadness to being happy and content with my life and circumstances, between envying those around me who had all their healthy children with them to feeling grateful for the healthy children I still had, and lastly, between existing and living.

One of the ways I was finally able to stop the madness of this destructive cycle was through rediscovering and accepting unconditional love. After going through such a sudden, traumatic loss, it was difficult to find love when I felt buried in tears, heartache, and overwhelming grief. Believe it or not, what helped me accomplish this initially was getting a dog. Dogs, unlike people, love and accept us exactly the way we are. They are always happy to see us, and they love us unconditionally. A few years ago I decided to get a puppy, Scout, and train her to become a therapy dog for the junior high school where I currently teach. Looking back on the therapy dog training, I now realize that it was Scout training me how to love again and how to heal my broken heart.

Scout, my yellow lab, has been going to school with me for almost two years now. She brings joy, smiles, happiness, and unconditional love to my students and our family every day. For dogs, love is an action word. It can become infectious if you allow it. I have learned so much from her about unconditional love, love that I had pushed to the back of the closet of my heart and tried to forget. After the loss of a loved one, God brings many different people, animals, and events into your life to carry you down your path of healing. Scout has become a stepping stone along my healing journey.

The best place to learn about unconditional love is from God. God loves us unconditionally, faults, flaws, sins, and all. The problem is, at the time you can be so overwhelmed with grief, it can become extremely difficult to see God working in your life in any way, shape, or form. Sometimes you cannot see that God has been walking with you all along. God does not abandon you, especially in your darkest hour. He is sitting there, quietly waiting for you to put down the tug-of-war rope and give Him the struggle instead. There is a Native American folktale that illustrates this exactly.

Cherokee Boy Becomes a Man

Do you know the legend of the Cherokee rite of passage?

His father takes him into the forest, blindfolds him, and leaves him alone. He is required to sit on a stump the whole night and not remove the blindfold until the rays of the morning sun shine through it. He cannot cry out for help to anyone. Once he survives the night, he is a man. He cannot tell the other boys of this experience because each lad must come into manhood on his own.

The boy is naturally terrified. He can hear all kinds of noises. Wild beasts must surely be all around him. Maybe even some human might do him harm. The wind blew the grass and earth, and shook his stump, but he sat stoically, never removing the blindfold. It would be the only way he could become a man. Finally after a horrific night, the sun appeared and he removed his blindfold. It was then that he discovered his father sitting on the stump next to him. He had been at watch the entire night, protecting his son from harm. We, too, are never alone. Even when we don't know it, our Heavenly Father is watching over us. When trouble comes, all we have to do is reach out to Him.

Moral of the story: Just because you can't see God, doesn't mean He is not there.

Author Unknown

10

THE EMPTY CHAIR

Change, like healing, takes time.

—Veronica Roth

After the death of my sister and the death of my daughter, holidays and birthdays were never the same. Nothing again would ever be balanced or happy for our family. How to handle holidays and birthdays after a loved one has died is often a very weighty decision, a dilemma in and of itself. Holidays and birthdays without your loved one are never-ending voids that never go away. There needs to be a *How To* book written for the ones left behind; unfortunately, it just isn't possible to write. Let me start by saying there is *no* right answer here. There is *no* one-size-fits-all in dealing with these milestone days without your loved one. The best advice I can give is to search your heart for the best way to proceed. You can also ask your surviving family members if they have any ideas on how to ease the pain of your loss during those special days that so loudly echo with emptiness.

I wrote often in my journal about the anticipation leading up to Mary's birthday and the holidays without her. Reading these journal entries can give a glimpse of how I dealt with the difficult task of facing special occasions without Mary. This journal entry was written right before we should have been celebrating her ninth birthday, our first birthday without her:

> *October 19, 2003: It is really hard anticipating your birthday. I am having a hard time remembering the feeling of your presence. I worry that as each day goes by, that puts me one day further away from the last day we spent with you. I don't ever want to forget, but it is so hard to find a balance between living now and remembering when. I feel that if I focus my full energy on either one, then I've lost the other completely.*

October 24, 2003, what should have been Mary's ninth birthday: Aunt Carrie, Uncle Erich, Katie and Joe came over for lunch. We put candles in the cupcakes and sang "Happy Birthday" to you. I hope you heard us! I took pumpkins that I decorated out to the cemetery. Oh, how words cannot describe how much we miss you today more than ever.

December 25, 2003, our first Christmas without Mary: Today is Christmas Day, and we all missed you. Both your brothers have been sick all week. It was hard to put on a happy face when all we wanted was to have you with us. Jeremy has been talking about you every day; I know he really misses you and just doesn't understand. It doesn't seem possible some days that this really happened. My heart aches to see you smile and hear you laugh. It just doesn't seem fair. Our family is so incomplete without you.

These journal entries echo the deep turmoil of dealing with the here and now, without getting stuck back in the how I wish it could still be. It is difficult to find a balance between remembering your loved one you miss so immensely and living in the moment to love the ones around you. These feelings are extremely intensified and challenging around the holidays. Pretending to be happy for the sake of your surviving loved ones can take a toll on you and bring you down even further. Do not be too hard on yourself during these difficult times, especially when going through your first year of holidays without your loved one. This is, by far, the most difficult of years, the year of firsts.

April 10, 2004, our first Easter without Mary: Today is Easter and it is our last holiday that we had with you last year. I still feel numb at the idea that you're not going to wear or need another new Easter dress or get up in the morning to find your Easter basket. I want so much to turn back the clock and have you here with us today. I had a really hard time sleeping last night; I just tossed and turned thinking about waking up without you. We went to Aunt Kris's for Easter dinner, and it just wasn't the same without you.

The bottom line when dealing with birthdays and holidays without your loved one is to just do the best you can. That is really all you can do. Early on, I drew strength from thinking about what Mary would have wanted me to do. I knew in my heart she would have wanted us all to celebrate and be happy, even without her here. I knew she was living happily in heaven, but the ache in my heart that first year and the years to come made it extremely difficult to function and be happy during the holidays. Again, adjusting to such devastating changes takes time, lots of time.

Perspective throughout my grief journey was imperative in keeping me on track to getting better, to healing, to moving on with my life, and accepting my new life for what it was. Keeping a healthy perspective is extremely difficult to do during the holidays. This particular journal entry gives a very poignant example of how perspective can mold you, shape you, make or break you.

Written about a year after Mary died: We went out for a special dinner tonight, just the four of us. I told your dad that it is so hard to understand how one can feel so alone without you with two other children right there. It was very strange tonight. They sat us at a table for five, so we sat through the whole meal with this empty chair. I think I am the only one who noticed. It is heart-wrenching to see such a visual reminder of your absence. Toward the end of the meal, I began to feel glad there was a chair there for you to join us. I know you weren't there, but it felt good to have this visual reminder of you. I love you, Mary, and I miss you terribly. You will always be my girl.

You can see how my perspective changed from the beginning to the end of our special night out. I went from focusing on the empty chair, to being glad it was there as a reminder of Mary. This perspective I am talking about takes work and time to achieve. It certainly does not happen overnight. Work at it slowly, and you will steadily begin to feel the bits and pieces of healing plant themselves into your heart. Look for opportunities to remember how blessed you were to have your loved one in your life, and search for small reminders that bring you comfort in the waves of grief that are bound to wash over you and consume you at times.

November 22, 2006, three and a half years after Mary died. Today is twenty years since my sister died, and I spent the day putting up Christmas decorations in our new house. It was a beautiful sunny day, and David and Jeremy had two friends over to play for the day. I couldn't help thinking and wondering how different my life would be with my sister in it. I still feel cheated that I never got to experience my adult life with my

> *sister. I also kept thinking about how Mary always loved to help me decorate for the holidays. How I ache and miss her every day. It is so hard to get ready for the holidays without her happy, excited spirit for the season. I want to wish her back so badly; I hate that I am losing what it feels like to have Mary here with us.*

You can sense from this journal entry the deep loss coming to the surface as I prepare for the coming holiday. It is so difficult not to focus on how it is supposed to be, instead of on the harsh cold reality of how it actually is.

Family traditions can be one way to help ease the pain of the holidays. Doing the same tradition without your loved one might be too painful for some. The bottom line is that it is up to you. One very special tradition that my family has—still to this day—that I deeply cherish is that every time we get together, we gather around in a circle, join hands, and pray. No matter how big or small the occasion, this circle of love is always a part of our time together. One special circle of love that is forever burned into my memory is when my daughter Mary died. We were at the funeral home and saying goodbye to Mary for the last time. As we finished saying our goodbyes, we formed a circle, touching Mary's coffin on each end, including her as part our circle, and we prayed. I know in my heart that Mary was smiling down from heaven, glad that our family circle and time of prayer tradition was including her and continuing in spite of the great heartache of the time. I am so thankful for this tradition of prayer and love in my family. Even though my sister, Mary K, and my daughter, Mary, are not physically with us, when we join hands and form a circle, I feel as if they are there, too.

11

A NIGHT AND DAY DIFFERENCE

*Whether we like it or not, men and women are not the
same in nature, temperament, emotions and emotional
responses.*

—J. Paul Getty

After Mary died, my husband and I started down two very separate paths of grief. Many people agree that men and women deal with various aspects of life in vastly different ways. We seem wired to think and respond differently in a number of situations life throws at us. This was especially true for my husband and me after our daughter, Mary, died. I went to grief group meetings, had quilts made out of Mary's clothes, often wrote in my journal, read lots of books about grief, and wanted to talk about Mary. I was also driven to find the answer to the haunting question of why Mary had died. Mary's father, Gregg, on the other hand, handled his grief much differently. He was more passive, was quiet much of time, and took comfort in keeping busy with work and doing jobs around the house.

Some may think when both parents experience the same loss, they should be able to support each other through the tragedy. This is extremely difficult to do, simply because both parents are essentially broken—their hearts are shattered, and at times they are barely able to sustain themselves through the loss. Those who can find a way to grieve together will have a much better chance of staying married. Grief is a problem with no immediate or even long-term solution. This poses a real challenge to all when faced with intense grief, but for men especially.

One specific memory I have about this major difference in how we approached our grief happened the day after Mary died. I recall standing in the family room of our home watching Mary's dad, grandpa, uncle, and cousin cut down a tree in our front yard. This may sound crazy to many, but at the time it made perfect sense to them. My family is in its fourth generation of operating a logging and sawmill business. The men in Mary's life felt utterly helpless to change the situation, so they did what they were most comfortable with and what made the most sense to them. They simply cut down a tree. The tree they cut down just so happened to be the tree that Mary was leaning against when she died. She was counting out her numbers in the game of tag she was playing. The tree was not at fault for anything; it just gave them a focus and something to do, since they were powerless to solve the real problem at hand. Only upon looking back am I able to understand their motive.

Another important memory I have about the differences between how we dealt with our grief happened while I was busy planning her memorial service with family and a few close friends. As we were discussing her service, Gregg adamantly stated that he was there the day Mary was born, and he was going to help carry her casket at her graveside burial service. Mary's dad had been so grief-stricken, he wasn't really able to help with the planning of her memorial service, but he saw an opportunity to *do something* with his grief that worked and held an important meaning for him. Planning her memorial service was not in him, but being a pallbearer for his only daughter was. Looking back, I have great admiration for the strength it must have taken for him to do this.

The summer after Mary died, I attended many grief support group meetings. I gained comfort from sharing my experience with others who understood more than most. It also gave me an outlet to talk about Mary, as I felt a deep desire and need to talk about her. Talking about Mary helped me feel as if she was still included in our family and in my life; for Gregg, talking about Mary was just too painful. I talked my husband into coming to one grief group meeting with me. In hindsight, I know it was too painful and way out of his comfort zone. It was the one and only time I ever heard him talk about riding in the helicopter with Mary to Children's

Hospital. I have to give him credit—he did try the grief group once. This is yet another example of how differently we grieved. What gave me an outlet sadly caused more pain and suffering for him.

When Mary died, our entire family balance went completely out of sync, like a car trying to run on three tires instead of four. Our family dynamic changed overnight: my boys no longer had their older sister to look after them, and Gregg and I could no longer share the parenting experience of raising our only daughter into adulthood. We spent a period of time after Mary's death tip-toeing around each other's suffering because we did not want to upset each other. If only we could have found a way to make a partnership in our grieving, sharing it in our own unique ways. This proved extremely difficult to do when we were both so broken inside.

In order to better understand the masculine side of grieving, I read the book *Swallowed by a Snake* shortly after Mary's death. Author Thomas Golden explains:

> *People naturally look for a safe place in which to experience the chaos of grief, but men and women tend to find safety in very different places. A woman often finds safety in her relationships with others and in relating the pain of her grief to those whom she is close. A man, on the other hand, does not see this kind of space as being particularly safe. He will tend (for many reasons) to seek a more private and action-oriented grief outlet. It is not, as many people think, that the man doesn't grieve. He merely seeks a different type of contained space.*

I learned the hard way that trying to get my husband to grieve my way was not the answer. I wanted to focus on working through our grief, and Gregg just wanted to take the focus away from it. I could not begin to understand, support, or empathize with Gregg's way of dealing with our loss any more than he could begin to understand, support, or empathize with my way. Sadly, a little over four years after Mary died, my husband and I divorced. Grief is so deeply personal and unique to each person, it becomes extremely difficult to understand another's pain, even the pain of a spouse. You do not have to grieve the same way; instead, you should respect each other's individual grief journey, as it is theirs and only theirs. This is overwhelmingly difficult to understand when you are in the midst of the grief storm yourself. It's sort of like being in the middle of a tornado and trying to jump rope at the same time.

Real grief healing has to come from within ourselves. Finding our way into the grief by using our strengths is the key, and each person's strengths are unique. Unfortunately, there is not someone or something out there that will be a quick fix in the grief healing journey or will give us the key to finding our strength.

12

JUST ONE WISH

A dream is a microscope through which we look at hidden occurrences in our soul.

—Erich Fromm

The dreams we have while we are asleep have deep meaning. Dreams are the subconscious mind at work, and they can have a very powerful effect on us. All of us, at some point in time, have awakened from a dream laughing or frightened. Dreams can be disturbing, romantic, fun, entertaining, frightening, and even bizarre. Dreams, when they are happening, are quite real. The motor that drives dreams is fueled by emotion. During the difficult days after my daughter Mary's death, I wrote in my journal about the dreams I had when I was lost, lonely, sad, grieving intensely.

> *August 29, 2003, four months after Mary died: Last night I dreamed that you were still here and that you had never died. It was all a mistake. In my dream I kept hugging you close and kissing you. I was also talking to you about how much I love you. You didn't say anything to me but just had that beautiful smile on your face. It was so nice to see you and hold you close to me. How I miss your hugs, your smile, and those beautiful brown eyes. What a beautiful little girl you were. I miss just having you near me to love and talk to. I always told you that I'd be heartbroken if something were to ever happen to you, and lately I've felt even more lost. I hurt so much inside that I feel like I don't want to go on some days.*

> *September 27, 2003, five months after Mary died: I've had a second dream about you. In the dream we were sitting on the floor in your room putting a puzzle together. I kept hugging you and kissing you. It was so nice to hold you close and see your beautiful face. In*

my dream we decided it was all a big mistake and that you were fine. You started to get weak, so I rushed you to the doctor, and she put you in a spring of life, and it cured you so you could live a long, healthy life. It was so hard when I woke up and realized that you were still gone. I miss you so much; it is like someone has punched me in the stomach.

Both of these journal entries encompass the deep and intense need to feel the loved ones we have lost. Losing the luxury we have every day—and even take for granted—of having our loved ones physically near us can at times make us feel overwhelmingly alone. Facing the harsh reality of knowing we will never get to hug, kiss, and touch the child, sibling, spouse, parent, or friend we have lost is by far the most difficult aspect of grieving. It is the punch in the gut that never goes away. It does dull with time, but it just does not end.

July 3, 2003, two months after Mary died: I dreamed you were at your baseball game, and we were in line to get some candy for a snack. You were happy and smiling and glad to see and be with me. I was so happy to put my arms around you and to touch your face. I even asked the lady working the concession stand if that was really you. When I woke up, I felt so glad that I got to see you and hold you close. I felt relieved that I had a dream about you. I miss you so much. It was so nice to see you and hold you close. I think the dream means that you think of me but you are happy.

May 6, 2004, one year after Mary died: I wanted to write down as I'm afraid I will forget the dream I had about Mary on the morning of Mother's Day. It was so nice to see Mary and have the sensation of her being near. The dream went something like this. We had found out by accident that Mary had the Long QT heart problem and she was put on medication. I remember that I just kept hugging her over and over telling her that I was going to make every minute count that we had with her. I actually felt happy when I woke up, which is a very rare thing. Mary looked really happy, but I don't remember her saying anything.

The common thread throughout these dreams is the desperate need to feel Mary's physical presence and to fix everything so she would be okay. Just being near Mary in my dream brought me both pain and comfort. You can almost feel the wishful thinking so painfully apparent in each dream I wrote about. Those of you who have lost a loved one undoubtedly get this. If you are new in your grief journey, I suggest you write down when you dream about the loved one you lost. Thirteen years later, I would never have remembered these dreams. Rereading my journal entries about the dreams I had about Mary bring me peace and comfort. I am so glad I wrote them down at the time.

I recently attended a funeral of a friend whose sister had died. The minister addressed this void of the physical presence we so desperately long for and hate facing the days ahead without. The pastor planted a seed of hope with the grieving family by telling them not to think about this as a goodbye, but instead as a *see you later.* As difficult as it can be, he suggested we not focus on the here and now, but on the eternity we get to spend in heaven forever with our loved one. Our time on earth is but a snapshot of the time we get to spend in heaven. Our brains are just not capable of comprehending the time span of eternity.

13

THE LEGACY

The two most important days in your life are the day you are born and the day you figure out why.

—Mark Twain

Soon after Mary died, I wrote an end-of-the-year tribute letter to my eighth grade language arts students. It included ideas, advice, insight, and wisdom to encourage them in their next four years of high school. I recently came across the letter. I have no idea how I wrote a letter like this just four weeks after Mary's death, other than to say God was working in and through me at the time. I had completely forgotten about this particular letter until I was searching for pictures to include on my son David's senior picture board.

End-of-the Year Tribute to the Class of 2007

There are so many things that I wanted to say to each of you, so I thought I would write this down and share some of my thoughts.

"It was the best of times, it was the worst of times, it was the season of light, it was the season of darkness, it was the spring of hope, it was the winter of despair, we had everything before us, we had nothing before us." This is a famous quote from the beginning of the book Tale of Two Cities, *by Charles Dickens. It sums up exactly how I feel about this school year, and explains how life is a complex combination of things. This has been a great year in so many ways, and, yet, it has been one of the worst years of my life. The class of 2007 will forever live in the memory of my mind and linger in the echoes of my heart. We both have a new world ahead of us; yours the start of your high school career, and mine is life without my daughter, Mary. You have all shown maturity beyond your years*

as you have reached out to support my family and me during this difficult time. I hope that this maturity will continue to grow and help you make wise choices as you begin high school.

I wanted to think of some good advice to share with you about how to be successful in high school, and my mind keeps going back to the life that my daughter lived in eight and a half short years, and the many lessons that I and so many learned from her. So, lessons from Mary are what I will be passing on to you.

Wisdom from an eight-year-old child: Mary K Elizabeth Butt

1. *Live life to the fullest and make every day count.*
2. *Show people you love them on a daily basis.*
3. *Smile. A smile is contagious, so share yours.*
4. *Always try to be helpful.*
5. *Treat others the way you want to be treated.*
6. *Don't be afraid to try new things.*
7. *You can do anything if you set your mind to it.*
8. *Open your heart to God.*
9. *Dream big dreams for yourself.*
10. *Never miss a photo opportunity.*

Looking at this list of things that Mary strived for makes me realize that each and every one of us can do so much with our lives if we set our minds in the right direction. Mary was far from perfect, as we all are, but

> *if we try to do just one of these each day, we can make
> a difference in our own lives and another person's life
> and not even know it. I would like to wish each one of
> you the best that life has to offer.*
>
> *Love,*
> *Barb Almendinger (Mrs. A.)*

You can see how, even early on in my grief journey, I was trying to find purpose amidst the immense sadness and overwhelming sea of grief I was drowning in. This letter I wrote to my students shows how each and every one of us has a purpose for living, a reason and a plan designed exactly for us. Some of us are able to fulfill our purposes in a short amount of time, and others are given many chances and lots of time to discover our purposes in life. We do not know why some of us are given a longer time on earth than others, but I do believe in my heart that when we get to heaven, we are going to suddenly realize there is no need to ask our long list of *why* questions. Just being in the presence of God will give us the understanding our earthly minds cannot possibly comprehend. I was stuck in the *why did this happen? why did Mary die so young?* phase for a very long time after her death. What I was eventually able to do was change the *why* to *what do I do now, God*, and move forward with my life.

> *October 6, 2003: Mary, the number of people who
> sent letters and cards was just overwhelming. You
> would not believe how many heart-warming notes I
> got that described the many ways you touched others,
> which even I didn't know about. From the girl you*

talked to on the bus to Mr. Hay, the school janitor. You reached out and touched the hearts of so many. The note from your gym teacher, Mr. Taylor, sounded just like you; reaching out to others less fortunate. I always knew you were an amazing little girl, but, oh, how I didn't really even know. I can imagine the glow you are now making in heaven and how proud God must be of you. You radiated joy and happiness and lived your life as an example for others. Thank you for touching so many and leaving your glow behind for us to smile and remember. I made many three-ring notebooks so that your brothers will better understand how special their big sister really was to so many. I love you, Mary, and will forever hold you close and dear to my heart. Love, Mom.

Reading this journal entry reinforces the reasons for living a life with purpose. You don't always realize how your actions impact a person; therefore, we need to strive to be kind to others in all situations. You can also see that reaching out to others in their time of grief can offer comfort and peace in the midst of a situation that is painfully impossible to endure. Sharing memories about the lost loved one with the bereaved can become a lifeline that means so much.

14

BUTTERFLY SIGNS?

The butterfly counts not months but moments, and has time enough.

—Rabindranath Tagore

Mary had a talent for drawing. The same year she died, she drew a picture of a beautiful yellow butterfly for her grandma's birthday gift. She spent hours looking at a picture I had on the wall of a butterfly and painstakingly drew every detail. She loved giving gifts to people, and couldn't wait to present her special butterfly drawing to her grandma. Her drawing is featured on the cover of this book.

A few days before Mary died, she discovered a badly injured yellow tiger swallowtail butterfly in our yard. Ironically, this is the exact type of butterfly she drew as a gift for her grandma. Being an avid animal lover, she marched into the house, butterfly held gently in her palm, and proceeded to do her best to try and save it. She retrieved a small Tupperware container, filled it with grass and a little water, and gently laid the butterfly on top of the small grass bed. She set this on her nightstand and was determined that she was going to be able to save this butterfly. Of course, it died. At the time I didn't think much about her quest to save this butterfly or the picture she drew. After her death, a completely different perspective of the butterfly she tried to save began.

How was it possible that Mary, without knowing the future, had this innate attraction to butterflies? Is there a message to be found here in the midst of the tragedy of a young child's life cut short? Was it possible that the death of the butterfly Mary tried to save was a foreshadowing of her own death? The butterfly, as I researched and discovered, is the symbol of the soul. Many people report seeing butterflies shortly after a loved one's death. Some see the butterfly as a symbol of resurrection, while others consider it to be the essence of the deceased's soul. Regardless of how you view butterflies, they do serve as important spiritual messengers.

Some people believe that "butterflies are God's confetti thrown upon the earth in celebration of His love," as the writer K. D'Angelo says. I happen to be one of them. The butterfly that was at the bottom of the "Footprints" poem I mentioned in Chapter 2 resonated loudly in my mind at the time of my daughter Mary's death. This poem had been hanging on the wall in my bedroom for almost twenty years; never did I imagine that this purple butterfly and all the butterflies I mentioned earlier in this chapter would later hold such importance in my healing. For after the deaths of two Marys, these butterflies took on an entirely new meaning.

People who experience great loss and intense pain in their lives go through something very similar to what a butterfly goes through. Think about it: A butterfly starts its life cycle as an egg; once the embryo has developed into a caterpillar, it emerges from the egg. The caterpillar typically sheds its skin and molts several times. It also can travel long distances in search of an ideal place to pupate. Once in the cocoon, a lot of changes take place, all in a very dark place. On the outside of the cocoon, there is no physical activity; all the change takes place on the inside. This stage of major change can last several months. Finally, the pupal stage is complete, and out emerges a beautiful butterfly.

When applying this to the life of a person who has gone through a tragic death of a child, parent, sibling, or spouse, this same concept of what the butterfly experiences rings true. We are the happy caterpillar, plugging along in life, oblivious of the darkness just ahead. When we lose our loved ones, we are plunged into a period of darkness, sorrow, loneliness, despair, and intense grief. In this time of darkness and grieving, we must do the work; no one can do it for us. This is the time when God is nearest to us, by our side, or carrying us if we can no longer walk. I am reminded of Mary Stevenson's "Footprints" poem: *He whispered, "My precious child, I love you and will never leave you never, ever during your trials and testing. When you saw only one set of footprints it was then that I carried you."* This is also when the greatest change can take place inside of us. If we allow God to dwell in our hearts and trust in Him through this time of intense darkness and sorrow, we can emerge from this part of our life renewed in our faith and love for Him.

The following story will help you see exactly what I am talking about. I'm sorry I don't know the author:

> *A man found a cocoon of a butterfly. One day a small opening appeared. He sat and watched the butterfly for several hours as it struggled to force its body through that little hole. Then it seemed to stop making any progress. It appeared as if it had gotten as far as it could, and it could go no further.*
>
> *So the man decided to help the butterfly. He took a pair of scissors and snipped off the remaining bit of the cocoon. The butterfly emerged easily. But it had a swollen body and small, shriveled wings. The man continued to watch the butterfly because he expected that, at any moment, the wings would enlarge and expand to be able to support the body, which would contract in time. Neither happened! In fact, the butterfly spent the rest of its life crawling around with a swollen body and shriveled wings. It never was able to fly. What the man, in his kindness and haste, did not understand was that the restricting cocoon and*

the struggle required for the butterfly to get through the tiny opening were God's way of forcing fluid from the body of the butterfly into its wings so that it would be ready for flight once it achieved its freedom from the cocoon.

Sometimes struggles are exactly what we need in our lives. If God allowed us to go through our lives without any obstacles, it would cripple us. We would not be as strong as what we could have been. We could never fly!

Do I think God placed the butterfly on Mary's heart to draw a picture of and try to save? Absolutely! I see God's handwriting all over it, and spiritual symbolism galore. The butterflies my sister and my daughter left behind give me a sense of hope and peace—hope that no matter how painful change can be for us, there is peace that God is always with us. His healing hands are ever-present. He never leaves us.

EPILOGUE

*Be a life long or short, its completeness depends on what
it was lived for.*

—David Starr Jordan

If you have not already noticed, my entire life story is just loaded
with coincidences. First the butterfly connection, then my sister
and my daughter are named Mary, and both die, seemingly healthy,
and at a young age. Finally, there is my journey to find out why my
daughter Mary died, which led to finding out why my sister Mary
died. On that journey I saved myself, when all I really wanted to
do is turn back the hands of time and save my daughter and sister.
I know how irrational that idea is, but when you are living deep
in the trenches of grief, nothing is logical or makes much sense.
Finding out the reason for my sister's death— seventeen years after
her death— was a relief, but it also brought the old grief back to the
surface.

My daughter, Mary, saved my life. Physically saved me. She only
lived eight and a half years, but her short life changed the lives of
my entire family forever. She not only saved my life, but the lives of
many in my family. Without her, we might never have known about
the silent killer lurking in so many members of my family, including

myself. This gift of life from such a giving, compassionate little girl is one that I know came straight from God. As Albert Einstein once observed, "There are two ways to live your life. One is as though nothing is a miracle. The other is as though everything is a miracle." Mary lives on. She is my family's everything miracle.

As I was in the process of writing this book, I lost my set of keys. I searched everywhere and, as I was emptying out my school bag, I came across the speech that I read at the memorial walk we had on the one-year anniversary of my daughter's death. Up until the day I had misplaced my keys, I had not laid eyes on this speech for over eleven years. It is no longer on a computer I have access to. It was purely God's plan that I found a copy of this speech to be able to share it. What follows is a powerful story that was enclosed in one of the cards I received after Mary's death. I used it to conclude the speech I read to some six hundred people who so willingly walked in the cold and rain in memory of Mary, May 3, 2004. I hope it touches your heart and gives you the same hope it has given me.

Eagles

Did you know that an eagle knows when a storm is approaching long before it breaks? The eagle will fly to some high spot and wait for the winds to come. When the storm hits, it sets its wings so that the wind will pick it up and lift it above the storm. While the storm rages below, the eagle is soaring above it. The eagle does not escape the storm. It simply uses the storm to lift it higher. It rises on the winds that bring the storm.

When the storms of life are upon us, we can rise above them by setting our minds and our belief toward God. The storms do not have to overcome us. We can allow God's power to lift us above them. God enables us to ride the winds of the storm that bring sickness, tragedy, failure, and disappointment into our lives. We can soar above the storms and use them to find a greater purpose for our lives. I encourage you to find purpose in your life deep within the storms.

Remember, it is not the burdens of life that weigh us down, it is how we handle them. The Bible puts it like this: *Those who hope in the Lord will renew their strength. They will soar on wings like eagles* (Isaiah 40:31).

APPENDIX

Following is a list of productive grief work I did. Some of these might help you rise like an eagle above the storm.

* Joined a grief support group for a short time after Mary died. This helped me to feel I wasn't alone, as our group shared some of the same or similar experiences as other people.

* Made scrapbooks with pictures of Mary and her brothers, one for David and one for Jeremy. Since my boys were so young, I knew they would have limited memories, if any, of their big sister. I wrote notes and stories about Mary in these scrapbooks, as I was worried I would forget them years later when the boys were old enough to appreciate them.

* Journaled by filling out a notebook called *Angel Catcher*. It is a place to write feelings and emotions about your loved one. It also helped me preserve my daughter's memory and gave me an outlet for many intense feelings about missing her.

*   Let balloons go on the anniversary of her death and on her birthday (with notes attached to the strings).

*   Made three quilts out of Mary's clothes. A dear friend who was talented at quilting hand-stitched hundreds of butterflies on three different quilts. She also sewed parts of Mary's clothes into each quilt. I also scanned Mary's signature and this same friend stitched it onto the quilts. I plan to give each of Mary's brothers a quilt when they graduate from high school as a gift in memory of their sister.

*   Had a bracelet made from a note that Mary wrote me. The note, complete with her first attempts at spelling, said, "Mom, hav a grt dy." Love Mary. I found a jeweler who could etch the words from the note into a silver bracelet, and I wear it every day. It helps to remind me how Mary wants me to have a great day, every day, even without her still here with us.

*   Some members of our church planted a garden in memory of Mary in the church flower beds.

*   Had a Mother's Ring made that included all three of my children.

*   Made many three-ring notebooks, which included the many letters and notes of encouragement people sent me after Mary died.

*   Had an auction to raise money for the Second Chance Humane Society since Mary was such an animal lover.

* Mary loved drawing, so I framed a few of her drawings and hung them on the wall.

* On the one-year anniversary of Mary's death, we had a fundraiser. We raised $12,000 to purchase defibrillators for many of the local schools. We made T-shirts for the walk with the image of Mary's butterfly drawing on the back.

* Planted a memory garden at Mary's elementary school. I still go every spring and fall and plant flowers there. We placed a rock in this garden that has the words, *Love to learn and learn to love,* etched onto it.

* Donated money to the local library since Mary loved to read. The staff used this money to make themed bags that people could check out. Each bag has a tag that says *Donated in memory of Mary K Elizabeth Butt.*

* Sent out Christmas cards for three years after Mary died that featured a picture she had drawn on the front of them. It was too difficult to send cards out and not include Mary's name, so this was my way of including her.

* Had a Christmas tree ornament made with Mary's picture on it.

* Invited Mary's second grade closest friends to pick an item from her bedroom as a keepsake to remember Mary.

* Had a necklace made with three charms on it. One charm has a miniature representation of Mary's footprints, another

has a note she wrote me that says, "Mom, I love you, Love, Mary," and the third charm has an etching of the butterfly Mary drew.

* Started collecting butterflies of all kinds.

* Gave college scholarship money to three students in Mary's class at what would have been her graduation in 2013.

* Bought a puppy and went through training classes so she could become a trained therapy dog.

* I also read many books. This is a list of the books that were most helpful:

A Grief Observed, by C.S. Lewis

When Bad Things Happen to Good People, by Harold S. Kushner

When There Are No Words, by Charlie Walton

The Empty Chair, by Susan J. Zonnebelt-Smeenge and Robert C. De Vries

The Bereaved Parent, by Harriet Sarnoff Schiff

I Wasn't Ready To Say Goodbye, by Brook Nowl and Pamela D. Blair

Water Bugs & Dragonflies, by Doris Stickney

Chad, by Dad

Gone but Not Lost, by David W. Wiersbe

Swallowed by a Snake, by Thomas Golden

Grace Disguised, by Jerry Sittser

Grace Revealed, by Jerry Sittser

CPSIA information can be obtained
at www.ICGtesting.com
Printed in the USA
FFHW020222160219
50572748-55902FF